First published by
Heritage Books in 1993
This revised edition 2000

Text by Pawlu Mizzi, BA, MQR

Edited by Louis J. Scerri, MA

Produced by
Mizzi Design & Graphic Services Ltd
Printed in Malta by
Gutenberg Press Ltd

Photography:
Daniel Cilia, Mario Mintoff
Department of Information
Malta Tourism Authority

Coat-of-Arms, Research, and Design:
Chev. Adrian Strickland

Acknowledgements:
Chev. Mgr. John Azzopardi; Alfred Baldacchino;
Chev Anthony Cassar de Saine; Chev John Critien; Dominic Cutajar;
Chev Roger De Giorgio, A&CE; Chev. Dr Philip Attard Montalto, LL.D.;
Ing. Richard Steeb, Chancellor of the Grand Priory of Austria
H.E. The Ambassador of the Sovereign Military Order of Malta Don Sforza Ruspoli;
The Office of the President of Malta;
The Embassy of the Sovereign Military Order of Malta accredited to Malta;
The Grand Priory of Austria for portraits of Grand Master Frà Galeazzo von Thun
und Hohenstein and Grand Master Frà Giovanni Battista Ceschi a Santa Croce;
The Maltese Association of the Sovereign Military Order of Malta;
The National Museum of Fine Arts, Valletta;
The Wignacourt Museum, Rabat, Malta

ISBN: 99909-75-68-X

THE ORDER OF ST JOHN

*T*he Order of Knight Hospitallers of St John has its origins in the early years of the first millennium AD. This was a time when the Christians were bent on getting control of the land where Christ was born, preached, and died, and of the churches built on sites intimately connected with His life as told in the Gospels.

These holy places had attracted pilgrims since the beginning of the spread of Christianity. A number had been destroyed or desecrated during Roman times, but they were later rebuilt and Christians continued to visit them regularly. When the Muslims took over Palestine Caliph Oman, Muhammad's first successor, laid a tax on Europeans visiting Jerusalem. Gradually Islamic harassment of Christians became greater. This led Pope Urban II to call on Christians at the Council of Clement in 1095 to give all they could to regain control of the Holy Land. Thousands rallied to the Pope's call and to the first Crusade which captured Jerusalem. The number of pilgrims increased and new rest houses and hospitals were needed.

Frà Gerard, founder of the Order, being led before the governor of Jerusalem accused of having thrown bread over the bastions to the besieging crusaders

Some generous merchants had already opened a few resting homes and had also built some churches. One of these was the Church of *Sancta Maria Latina* near the Garden of Olives. Beside this church, in which liturgy was celebrated in the Roman rite (hence the name *Latina),* the Benedictines, with the help of some merchants from Amalfi, built a hospital known as the *Sacra Domus Hospitalis* which catered for male pilgrims. A hospice for females, attached to the church of *Sancta Maria Magdalena,* was also built.

The Benedictines needed many nurses to help them run the two places. Between 1008 and 1028 Father Simon of Syracuse, *capo ospitaliere dei pellegrini di Terrasanta,* organized these nurses and formed them into a sort of congregation infusing into them the Benedictine spirit of hospitality. Their patron saint was to be St John the Baptist.

The group carried on for some time. When they had to cut themselves off from the Benedictines, Brother Gerard and a number of his colleagues asked Pope Paul II to recognize them as a religious order of lay hospitallers under the protection of the Holy See. They requested the right to own property and be exempted from paying tithes and other dues to bishops. On 15 February 1113 the Pope granted the request and approved their rule. At first they did not take the vows of religious orders but later on these became obligatory. The Pope gave them the right to possess lands, buildings, convents, and hospitals anywhere.

When Brother Raymond du Puy (or Puis) succeeded Bro. Gerard, he began to be called *Maestro dello Spedale* together with the title of Rector or Governor. Raymond called a General Chapter of all the members at which the Order was given new ideals. To the religious and nursing duties were added the chivalric ones of defending the Holy Land and the pilgrims from infidels and thieves.

1

Members of the Order restoring the walls of Jerusalem following the attack on it in 1229 by Muslim fanatics. Rinaldo of Haifa, governor of the city (extreme right), being advised on the work by the military engineer of the Order. Fresco by Perez d'Aleccio at the Grand Masters Palace in Valletta

In 1177 their leader, Roger de Moulins, assumed the title of Grand Master.

In 1259 Pope Alexander IV gave them as their particular dress the black mantle of the Benedictines on which they were to carry a white eight-pointed cross symbolizing the eight beatitudes.

The Order of the Knight Hospitallers remained in Jerusalem until Saladin took the city in 1187. They, then, went to Acre, but only after a siege lasting three years. In 1291 Melemuk of Egypt ousted them from the Palestinian mainland and they went to Limassol in Cyprus. The naval aspect of the Order has its origins in these days when they

Mohamet I (stick in hand) leading the siege on Rhodes between 23 May and 27 July 1480, during which the knightly banners and gonfalons with the images of the Virgin and St John appear to have frightened the Turks and routed them away. Grand Master Pierre D'Aubusson was also miraculously healed from a mortal wound he had received in the chest. From a fresco by Perez d'Aleccio at the Grand Masters Palace in Valletta

had to build warships of all sorts and have a fleet of their own. In 1310 the knights conquered Rhodes and settled on the island until they were defeated by Suleiman II in 1522.

For seven years Grand Master L'Isle Adam roamed around Europe requesting help and a roof from Christian kings and princes. The Order was offered Cerigo (or Cytheres) in Morea and Elba but both were refused because they belonged to the Venetians who were friendly to the Turks due to commercial interests. Suda in Crete was also turned down because its owner, the Prince of Piombino, asked for a huge sum. The islands of Minorca, Ischia, and Ponza were also refused, as also the suggestion to set house in Malta when it had been discussed by the grand master and the Sicilian Viceroy, Ettore Pignatelli.

Bosio says that on 17 June 1524, L'Isle Adam received in Viterbo the Dominican Archbishop of Capua, Nicolò Scambergo, a close friend of Pope Clement VIII, who was returning from a mission of mediation between Emperor Charles V of Spain and King Francis I of France. Following this meeting Scambergo seems to have recommended the pope's intervention in favour of the Order taking Malta. Charles V accepted on condition that the Knights were (a) to be also responsible for the defence of Tripoli (b) to be perpetual feudal lords and not

Grand Master Frà Philippe de Villiers de l'Isle Adam accompanied by his faithful hospitallers leaving the island of Rhodes on 1 January 1523. Fresco by Perez d'Aleccio at the Grand Masters Palace, Valletta

sovereigns, and as a manifestation of this, were to send every year a falcon to the viceroy of Sicily; and (c) not to let ships of nations, considered to be at war with Spain enter the harbours.

These conditions went directly against the sovereign and neutral nature of the Order and the knights, although in the worst possible state, could not accept them. There were even those who, on hearing the conditions being read out to them, shouted, 'Burn that document.'

Meanwhile the grand master and the Order's Council did not lose heart and in December 1525 they asked Charles V for permission to send a delegation to Malta, Gozo, and Tripoli after which they would give a reply. The commissioners reported that (a) if the Order were to take Malta and Tripoli it would have to build fortresses, bastions, buildings, and houses for the knights and for the people, because their towns and villages were practically base; (b) both Malta and Tripoli were too open to attack and difficult to defend in case of siege from all sides; (c) the Order would have to provide food because the land did not bear much fruit and entries from custom duties were low; and (d) it was impossible to keep the canal between Malta and Tripoli closed to enemy ships in order to defend Christian forces.

This report was not received very enthusiastically. The Spanish knights wrote to their emperor explaining their plight. The Prior of Capua, Julian Riddo, was sent to Pope Clement to ask him to intercede on the Order's behalf so that Charles would better the conditions for the lease of the island. But even the pope's intervention was to no avail. Charles V, like Alphonse the Magnanimous before him, was anxious to rid himself of the responsibility of defending Malta and Tripoli, but he would not budge and since the begging knights could not but choose to accept his offer, on 23 March 1530, at Castelfranco near Bologna, he signed the lease of Malta to the Order entrusting it also with the defence of the castle and town of Tripoli. L'Isle Adam signed the deed of acceptance on 25 April 1530.

It seems that the emperor granted the knights' requests that (a) Malta and Tripoli should pass to them as free feuds without any signs or symbols of serfdom except the annual donation at a simple ceremony of a falcon *'in maniera de perpetua memoria de tal beneficio receputo'*; (b) the inhabitants should not be under the direct rule of the Sicilian viceroy but should nonetheless receive grain from Sicily without paying custom duties; and (c) the Order would continue to mint its own currency.

The news of the transfer of power had a mixed reception in Malta. The island's nobility were alarmed at the thought that the knights, belonging to the elite of Europe's aristocracy, would deprive them of their former powers as leaders of the people. So also were the higher ranks of the clergy who saw even greater rivalry from the members of a religious military Order. Both classes had their centre of influence at Mdina. The people of Birgu (the second most important town and located on the harbour), among which were many of Spanish and Sicilian origin if not by birth, were, however, overjoyed because the presence of the rich sea-faring knights would create commerce, work, and wealth and provide defence against Muslim corsairs together with care of the poor and the sick. It also meant for them a diminution of the powers of the rival city of Mdina and its rich nobles.

In actual fact the Maltese never had any official intimation of what was going on. The Council of the *Università*, after several meetings and prolonged discussions, decided on 10 April 1524 to send Giacomo Inguanez, Toni Bonello, and Alvaro Casseres to the viceroy of Sicily to claim that the transactions being effected over their heads constituted a breach of the liberties, rights and privileges which the Maltese had bought when they paid the ransom to Monroi. Duke Ettore Pignatelli made short shift of the delegation on the pretext that matters were at such a premature stage that it was too early to take heed of rumours. The representatives did not realize that they were being tricked and on their return to Malta the *Università* and the people took their assurances for granted and did not prepare themselves for resistance to imposition as had been done on similar occasions in the past.

When the Bailiff of Monoasca, Giovanni di Boniface, as representative of Grand Master *L'Isle Adam*, took the oath confirming the knights' acquiescence to Charles V's demands, it was only witnessed by the representatives of Spain and of the Order; the Maltese were not aware of what was happening.

Soon after, on 10 June 1530, the bailiff came to Malta with three ships, the *Capitana*, the *S. Giovanni*, and the *S. Filippo*. He landed at Birgu and went directly to Mdina. The *Capitano della Verga* and the jurors P. de Nasis, A. Rapa, and L. Baglio had called the *Consiglio Popolare* to draw up the list of rights, privileges, and immunities which was to be presented to the Order. The Maltese also asked that (a) the amount of money they had paid to Monroi be deposited by the Order with the *Regia Curia* so that Malta would still have the right to form part of the *Regio Demanio* and return to its former status if the knights left; and (b) if the Order minted its own currency, this would not be of any prejudice to the Maltese receiving grain from Sicily without paying customs duties. The Maltese claims do not seem to have been too effectively presented. In fact the 30,000 florins, instead of being deposited with the Royal Court, were given as a gift to the emperor and to the Order.

The grand master landed at Birgu on 26 October 1530 but it was not before 30 November that he took the oath, on a cross the knights had brought with them from Rhodes, that the Order would confirm the privileges and customs of the island. On their part the Maltese did not pass over the two silver keys of Mdina before he had taken the oath. The symbolic presentation of the keys was made by the *Capitano della Verga*. Bosio says that after the ceremony L'Isle Adam entered the capital under a canopy amid clapping, fireworks, and the ringing of bells.

Notwithstanding all promises the first acts of the Order showed its autocratic nature. The grand master, in fact, on the pretext of a better administration of the island, divided Malta into two parts and left the *Capitano della Verga* in apparent control of the old capital while he set up a new *Università* for Birgu, l-Isla, Bormla, Żejtun, Gudja, Żebbug, and Qormi, practically the whole of the harbour area.

Very soon another problem cropped up. It had always been the privilege of the *Universitas* to present nominations for the bishop of Malta. Charles V transferred this right to the Order on the excuse that the bishop had to be a person who had to enjoy the pleasure of the Order. And henceforth, notwithstanding the protests of the Maltese, the knights would send three names (among which there always had to be a Spaniard or a Sicilian) to the Spanish emperor who would then pass on for confirmation by Rome the one he chose.

Abstract from Andrew Vella Storja ta' Malta, *Vol. I, 182-5*

REFERENCES:
M. Mignot, *Histoire de l'Empire Ottoman*. Paris 1771.
G.Bosio, *Dell'Istoria della Sacra Religione et Illma. Militia di San Giovanni Gierosolimitano*, Rome, 1594

PHILIPPE VILLIERS DE L'ISLE-ADAM
1521-1534

*A*t the time of the cession of our islands to the Order of St John of Jerusalem, the grand master was Philippe Villiers de L'Isle-Adam, a Frenchman and perhaps the most remarkable head the Hospitallers ever had.

He reached Malta from Syracuse with his knights on the morning of 26 October 1530 and soon set his residence and the seat of the Convent at Birgu. On 13 November he proceeded in a solemn procession to Mdina where he was met at its gate by the jurats and, after renewing his oath 'to observe and command the observance of all the privileges and all the graces granted to the island by the Invincible Kings of Aragon and Sicily', he received the keys of the city from the *capitaneo*, Paolo de Nassis, thus, putting him in possession of the island.

His first care was to fortify Birgu which he enclosed within a wall, flanked by a small bastion to secure it against any assault. He also built a palace which continued to be the residence of his successors until the time of La Valette.

He also set up a sound administration. He divided the island of Malta into two cantons: one comprising the city of Notabile and the parishes of Naxxar, Birkirkara, Siggiewi, and Żebbuġ, which he placed under the administration of the *Capitano della Verga*; and the other, including Birgu, the parishes of Żejtun, Żurrieq, Qormi, Gudja, and the adjoining districts, which were placed under the civil jurisdiction of a magistrate chosen by the grand master. The creation of this new official, who shared the administration of the island with the captain of the city, was the first assault upon the rights of the people. He, then, appropriated himself of the custom duties which the *Universitas* had been authorized to impose by the king of Sicily and increased them.

The *universitas* of Malta and Gozo deeply resented this usurpation of their rights and privileges, and made remonstraces before the Council of the Order. But their complaints served no purpose.

On 5 September 1533 L'Isle-Adam promulgated a body of laws which chiefly dealt with criminal matters under the title Statues and Ordinances.

He died at Rabat on 22 August 1534, and was buried in the chapel of Fort St Angelo.

PIETRO DEL PONTE
1534-1536

L'Isle-Adarn was succeeded on 26 August 1534 by Pietro del Ponte, a Piedmontese, a man of austere manners and a zealous observer of discipline. He assumed the government of the island on 10 November.

Although hardly settled in his post, del Ponte later joined Charles V in an expedition against Tunis, where the formidable corsair, Ariadeno Barbarossa (Hair-ed-din) had dethroned Muley Hassan and placed the city under the suzerainty of the Porte. The Maltese participation was made up of the *gran carracca*, three galleys, and 18 smaller vessels with some 2,000 soldiers. They fought with great bravery and showed that the Order had not lost the military valour for which it was so greatly renowned. The victory of the Christians was complete. Barbarossa was defeated and Muley Hassan reinstated. He, consequently, acknowledged himself the vassal of Spain, and while re-opening his ports up to the emperor, he secured the former possessions of the Hospitallers in Barbary, thus extending North African commerce to the island. Five years later Barbarossa regained Tunis.

In 1535 famine struck the island compelling the grand master and the Università to solicit the importation of a greater quantity of corn than ordinary from Sicily. The request was granted, but not so fully as to satisfy the needs of the island. In the following year, in fact, it was felt necessary to decree the forced sale of grain upon the Sicilian vessels in port. This step which gave rise to a very serious dispute between the *Università* of Messina and that of Malta.

Del Ponte's short period of rule did not permit him to introduce any changes in the administration of the island.

The grand master died on 18 November 1535 and was buried in the chapel of St Angelo by the side of L'Isle Adam.

DIDIER DE SAINT JAILLE
1535-1536

*O*n 22 November 1535 a Frenchman, Didier de Saint Jaille, held in esteem for his great prudence, was raised to the office of grand master. His valour during the siege of Rhodes brought him to the forefront in the Order's top hierarchy. His name had for a long time been synonymous with gallantry. He received news of his election while he was in France.

During Saint Jaille's brief grandmastership, the knight Jacques Pelliquen, who acted as lieutenant of the Order, had to take the important decision of attacking and destroying El Haid Tower near Tripoli. The Muslim corsair, who commanded it, was a daredevil, equal in courage to Barbarossa but a hundred times more cruel. The attack was carried out with complete success by 700 Maltese and Calabrian soldiers and 150 knights led by the knight Bottigella. In the fierce battle which ensued, Chasse-Diable, as the corsair was also called, was mortally wounded and his troops routed.

As the news of the knights' successes spread all over the island, two episodes marred the general happy atmosphere. A young novice, who had aspired to the chaplaincy of the Order, robbed the precious stones which had adorned the image of Our Lady of Philermos brought some years earlier from Rhodes. Some days later an English knight stabbed a Maltese girl because of jealousy. Both offenders were condemned to death.

During his reign de Bourbon, grand prior of France, ordered a hanging of tapestry on silk embossed with gold bearing the effigies of the grand masters as they appeared on originals brought from Rhodes.

He soon made preparation for his return but on the way back he fell ill at Montepellier and died on 26 September 1536 before reaching the island.

JUAN D'OMEDES
1536-1553

*O*n 20 October 1536 an Aragonese, Juan D'Omedes, was elected grand master. He was grasping and ambitious and, like ambitious people, generally of a cruel disposition.

He made it his constant aim to dominish the powers of the Maltese *Universitas*. Using the pretext that Notabile was a long distance away from other urban centres in the south, he instituted a second comune at Birgu which, wholly subject to his will, administered the affairs of the southern canton of the island. He took the command of the coast guards from the captain of the city and handed it over to the seneschal, a dignitary of the Order. He also imposed new taxes and reduced salaries. The leaders of the Maltese again appealed to the emperor against the bad government of the grand master, but it was all in vain for Charles V, finding in D'Omedes a man after his own heart, encouraged his hateful innovations according to the statutes of the Order.

Charles V allowed D'Omedes to coin money, a privilege previously denied to Saint Jaille. Also, he forced him in disastrous enterprises in Africa. In retaliation, the corair Dragut (Rais Torghud), the terror of navigation, landed unexpectedly in Gozo twice during the rule of this grand master. The first time he carried off fifty prisoners without encountering any resistance. The second time in 1551 he carried away into slavery almost all the inhabitants of the island. Then, he proceeded to Tripoli which he reconquered for Suleiman.

D'Omedes, then, decided to strengthen the fortifications of Malta. He decreed the erection of two forts, one upon St Elmo point and the other upon

Monte San Giuliano. In the matter of legislation D'Omedes promulgated six ordinances of little or no importance. After seventeen years of miscalculation and misconduct, Grand Master D'Omedes died on 6 September 1553.

CLAUDE DE LA SENGLE
1553-1557

*T*he long and unfortunate rule of D'Omedes led to the election, on I I September 1553, of Claude de la Sengle, a knight of the langue of France, renowned for his great judgement, virtue, and bravery. At the time of his election La Sengle was ambassador of the Order at the court of Pope Julius III, so that the new grand master did not arrive in Malta till the following January.

In dealing with the rights and prerogatives of the *Universitas*, he followed in the footsteps of his predecessors: he deprived the natives of the command of the militia to bestow it upon his knights, he imposed new burdens, and he attempted to tax landed property. But so weighty was the opposition he encountered that he had to abandon his design.

On the other hand, he provided for the defence of the island and made it much stronger to resist the attacks of the ever-dreaded Turk. He made Fort St Michael a new city to which was given his own name, Senglea. Soon after his election, the grand master was offered the city of Afriqiya. But he refused it because of lack of funds for maintaining its population and fortifications. The situation became more precarious when in October 1555 a heavy storm destroyed almost the entire fleet and about 600 of his ablest men and 40 knights were lost. He also extended the fortifications of Birgu, deepened the moats around it, and increased the number of its dwellings so that it was called Città Nuova, a name which it preserved for a few years. He also added and completed other works of public utility which had been begun by his predecessors. In 1555 he published some criminal laws which bear the stamp of his time.

He died at Notabile on 18 August 1557, leaving the Order a rich patrimony. He was buried in the chapel in St Angelo. His heart was buried in the church of the Annunciation, outside Rabat.

JEAN DE LA VALETTE
1557-1568

*J*ean de la Valette, a knight of the langue of Provence, was proclaimed grand master on 21 August 1557. He was a strong man, full of valour and enthusiasm.

The new grand master was determined to consolidate the Order's rule on the island. He first silenced in a ruthless manner all opposition of the Maltese, sending to the gallows patriots like Mattew (Giuseppe) Callus, who was one of its leaders. He then deprived their *Universitas* of many of its rights. He also tried to cut their connection with Sicily.

One of his first acts was to obtain from Philip II of Spain the right of deciding feudal disputes in the tribunals of the Order. Besides, he was exempted from requesting investiture from the viceroy, thus freeing the Order from the interference of royal ministers in Sicily (1558).

La Valette, however, had other more problems threatening him. Tripoli was one of these. La Valette, thus, induced Philip to attempt its reconquest (1559). The enterprise was entrusted to the Duke of Medina Ceti, viceroy of Sicily. But the Christian armada was defeated near Djerba (1560).

Another problem was the thorny relationship between State and Church on religious matters. Twice during the rule of La Valette, the Congregation of the Holy Office unsuccessfully tried to establish the tribunals of the Inquisition in Malta.

Meanwhile, the knights having seized the *Gran Sultana*, Suleiman declared war on the Order. On 18 May 1565 some 138 galleys under the command of Pialì Pasha landed in Malta a force of 40,000 men commanded by Mustapha Pasha. For almost four months they besieged the island. Then, on 6 September, the Turkish armada mysteriously left Malta, giving La Valette the glory of a great victory.

The victory inspired La Valette to build a fortified city on Mount Sceberras which had been planned for some time. Funds were provided maninly from Pope Pius V and Philip of Spain. The plan was by Francesco Laparelli. On 28 March 1566 La Valette laid the first stone of the new city, which was called Valletta.

The heroic Grand Master died on 21 August 1568. He was buried in the church of Our Lady of Victories in the new city.

PIETRO DEL MONTE
1568-1572

*P*ietro del Monte, an Italian, succeeded La Valette on 23 August 1568. He made it his chief duty to continue the project of the newly founded city. For this purpose he raised a loan at Palermo on the commanderies of Italy and Spain; and, with the consent of the *Consiglio Popolare*, he imposed a new duty upon corn. Besides, in order to ensure that buildings were built according to approved plans, he also appointed a commission to draw up the *Regolamenti sulle Case*. This commission suggested the division of the new city into two parts; that is, the *collacchio* and the *fuori di collacchio*. The suggestion was not adopted – either because it was deemed desirable to leave the choice of sites free so that the city should be built up more quickly or because the people regarded the division unfavourably as an odious distinction between the knights and the Maltese.

During the magistracy of Del Monte, Selim, the successor of Suleiman the Great, attacked Cyprus and took Nicosia, Paphos, and Limassol. In retaliation the major Christian powers resolved to unite in common defence. Marc'Antonio Colonna commanded the papal galleys while Andrea Doria, the Sicilian, led the Venetian galleys as well as those of Malta and of all the Italian republics. Don John of Austria was commander-in-chief. A great battle was fought in the Gulf of Lepanto on 28 October 1571.

On the invitation of the pope, all Christendom was asked to recite the rosary at the time of the battle. The Maltese, led by Chev. Gregorio Carafa, were the first to go into this attack. The struggle was tough but it ended in a complete victory for the Christian powers, who for the first time were united in a common enterprise.

That same year Del Monte moved the seat of the Convent from Birgu to Valletta and, a year later, under the direction of the engineer Girolamo Cassar, he began the building of the Grand Masters' Palace.

He confirmed the *Regolamenti sulle case* promulgated by his predecessor and enjoined their observance. He also instituted laws of a penal character.

He died on 26 January 1572 and was buried in the church of Our Lady of Victories.

JEAN L'EVESQUE DE LA CASSIÈRE
1572-1581

*O*n 30 January 1572, Jean de la Cassière, a Frenchman and a man of austere religious disposition, was proclaimed as Del Monte's successor.

The exhausted Treasury and the double necessity of pushing on with the building of the city and providing for the defence of the island still actively threatened by the Turks, obliged the new grand master to raise loans by mortgages on the property of the Order and to impose fresh taxes. He also tried to compel the bishop to pay the royal tribute which formerly used to be paid to the kings of Sicily, but without success, as immunity from such payment had been granted to the Bishop by Ferdinand the Catholic and confirmed by Rome.

La Cassière also paid for the building of the conventual church of St John's, desiggned by the Maltese engineer Girolamo Cassar. It was consecrated by the archbishop of Palermo on 20 February 1578.

He reformed the tribunals and issued laws of a penal and administrative character. Because of such reforms the grand master and Bishop Gargallo were often at loggerheads. When relations were eventually brought back to normal the Holy Office of the inquisition was established in the island. The brief was published in Malta on 8 August 1574 and the inquisitor began to exercise his jurisdiction soon after.

In 1581 a lamentable scarcity of food became the cause of further rifts between Church and State. The grand master was accused of foresight and on 6 July some knights declared him unfit to govern. They even slandered him and, after imprisoning him in Fort St Angelo, they appointed Chev. Romegas as a lieutenant in his stead.

The Maltese took the side of the grand master. They sent him word with the captain of the city offering him to raise 2,000 armed men to assist him as soon as he ordered them. He prudently declined the offer, saying that he looked for justice from the supreme head of the Order. In fact, Gregory XIII, who had a very great regard for La Cassière, sent Mgr. Venosti to Malta to recall both the grand master and his lieutenant to Rome. La Cassière was honourably received at Rome, and his innocence fully vindicated.

He died in Rome on 21 December 1581 but his remains were transported to Malta and buried in the conventual church of St John's.

HUGUES LOUBENX DE VERDALLE
1582-1595

*B*ecause of dissension among the knights, fears were entertained that the Council might make a bad choice. Requests were therefore made to Pope Gregory XIII to appoint the successor to La Cassiere. This the pontiff declined to do, but he proposed three candidates to the Council: Penisses, Moreton, and Verdalle. Of these the council elected Verdalle on 12 January 1582.

At that time the islands were still threatened by the Turks, and although these once-formidable enemies were no longer in a position to undertake great enterprises, the grand master insisted on stronger fortifications stocked with sufficient munitions of war and provisions. In 1584, following the sacking of Gozo by four galleys of Bizerta during which 70 persons were carried off, Verdalle decided to build a fort on Comino which had been contemplated for some time. For this purpose he proposed a tax upon articles of food in that island to which the Gozitans willingly agreed.

The plans for better fortifications did not, however, help to relieve the awkward social conditions on the island. In 1591 the increase of the population and the scarcity of food led to famine and the year after the island was ravaged by a pestilence.

Verdalle continued in the arrogance of his predecessors in depriving the Maltese commune of its rights and prerogatives. His despotism was, however, of an enlightened kind. He decreed laws for the public safety, protected agriculture, and showed his interest in education by establishing a college in Valletta under the direction of the Jesuits.

Even then there were those who regarded the introduction of the Jesuits as a mistake, alleging that they were an ambitious body of men who, by the influence they exercised over their pupils in their studies, turned the minds of young men away from the profitable pursuit of seamanship.

In the last years of Verdalle's rule the dissensions and rivalries in the convent greatly increased. In spite of his status – being formerly created a cardinal of the Church by Pope Sixtus V – he was accused in front of Pope Clement VIII, who was not very friendly to him, of malpractices, injustice, and nepotism.

Weighed down by disease and the mortifications to which he had been subjected, he breathed his last on 4 May 1595.

MARTIN GARZES
1595-1601

*M*artin Garzes of the langue of Aragon was elected grand master on 8 May 1595. Sicily, then belonging to Spain, naturally favoured a grand master of Spanish nationality. To compliment the Order's choice, Philip II decreed an increased supply of grain for our population thus easing the scarcity of food which had been so keenly felt under Verdalle. The king also gave the Order with 40,000 crowns to help in fortifying Gozo.

Garzes was reputed to have been very sympathetic with the Maltese. He understood many of their worries but after he became grand master he lifted no finger restore to the commune the rights and prerogatives taken by his predecessors. However, he did not continue the usurpation. He devoted a great deal of his time and money to the development of Valletta, which he knew offered a wider field to industry and commerce than any other city. He was conscious at the same time of the threat that Notabile could consequently suffer at the expense of further urbanization. To guard against the depopulation of this old city, the grand master granted its inhabitants a number of privileges. Chief among these was the right to recourse to his own tribunals in civil and criminal matters. They were also allowed to appeal to their own magistrate in criminal cases, and to be exempted from obligatory military service.

Garzes also showed great consideration for the safety of the Maltese. He built St Martin (Garzes) tower in Gozo and planned other coastal towers to increase security and set up institutions to care for the poor and the needy. On the initiative of Commandant Emanuele Quiros, a Portuguese, he instituted the *Monte di Pietà*. In the general chapter held on 4 January 1598 to consider how to save the poor from the exaction of Turkish and Jewish usurers, he also offered 2,000 crowns of his own money for this purpose and demanded that the Common Treasury should contribute at least another thousand.

Garzes' grandmastership, was, however, to be marked with continuous dissent between the various classes of society. As soon as the members of the Convent ceased to quarrel among themselves, the situation was bedevilled with jurisdictional conflicts. Serious differences arose between the Order's court and the tribunal of the Inquisition and also sometimes that of the bishop. Appeals to Rome went on uninterruptedly, thus alienating the people from the real social and economic problems.

After nearly six years of just rule, Garzes died on 7 February 1601.

ALOF DE WIGNACOURT
1601-1622

*A*t a meeting held on 10 February 1601 Alof de Wignacourt of the French langue was elected grand master.

The population continued to increase notwithstanding early deaths from pestilence and famine and the continuous enslavement of whole families during the frequent raids by Barbary corsairs. This problem was further increased by shortages of food supplies from Sicily which could be hardly compensated with the booty captured by the Order and other privateers in the Mediterranean.

To put a check upon the abuses resulting from the great number of armed privateers in the island, the grand master appointed a commission to inquire into this state of affairs and suggest the necessary remedies. On receiving the report of the commissioners, he appointed on 17 June 1605 the *Magistrato degli Armamenti* to take cognisance of disputes between privateers. He also forbade privateering under whatever flag except under certain conditions and with a caution not to molest the vessels of Christian princes. He finally demanded a tenth of all the booty taken by foreign vessels and conveyed to Malta to be sold or divided.

Wignacourt also established the *Monte della Redenzione*. Although only poorly managed at first, this institution acquired much greater means in the course of time through the legacies of private persons. Every Easter it was able to ransom a good number of Christian slaves.

Among the various works done by this grand master the most important was the aquaduct from outside Rabat to Valletta. This was began in 1610 under the direction of the Jesuit Tomasucci and was completed in 1615 under the direction of Bontadini, a Bolognese engineer.

Like his immediate predecessor, Alof de Wignacourt reduced the *Universitas* to the shabby state in which Verdalle had left them. In spite of this, the Maltese valued his sense of justice and munificence.

Verdalle, also, often clashed with the inquisitor over temporal matters relating to members of the Order. Out of regard for Wignacourt, Ferdinand II conferred the title of Most Serene Highness upon him and successive grand masters. This conferment was the cause of great antagonism between grand master and inquisitor, who wished to be styled Most Illustrious, a title which the council granted to him and to all the grand crosses of the Order.

When Alof de Wignacourt died on 14 September 1622, he was sincerely lamented by all.

LUIS MENDES DE VASCONCELLOS
1622-1623

*L*uis Mendes de Vasconcellos, of the langue of Castille, on succeeding to Wignacourt on 17 September 1622, showed that he wanted to restore the rights and prerogatives to the *universitas* which his predecessors had long deprived them of. He would probably have succeeded had he not been so advanced in age.

Although Vasconcellos announced his intention to carry out the projects of his predecessor, the council did not always share his opinion. The island of Cornino, according to the councillors, belonged to the Order and not to the grand master. Consequently they annulled the provision in Wignacourt's will by which an annual impost of 800 crowns was to be levied upon that island for the maintenance of the aqueduct, the fortifications, and other works of public utility.

Vasconcellos' short grandmastership would have ended almost uneventfully had he not come to loggerheads with Bishop Cagliares over the building of an episcopal palace in Valletta. Versions about the causes of the differences between Vasconcellos and Cagliares differ. Some hold that they were product of senility arising from baseless doubts that a bishop's court in Valletta could be a threat to the civil administration of the Order. Others blame Cagliares's ambition and tenacity in his vision of a Church that was not inferior to the State, either spiritually or temporally. The palace was, in fact, a symbol of status and its absence in administrative cities could not be tolerated by ecclesiastic authorities. The issue could have also been deliberately exaggerated by the Order's dignitaries close to the grand master who were antagonistic to Cagliares because of his Maltese descent. Baldassare Cagliares was, in fact, the only Maltese ecclesiastic to be appointed bishop during the Order's rule in Malta. In spite of all opposition, however, Cagliares proceeded with his plan of building his palace in Valletta. Vasconcellos asked and obtained an inhibitory order from Rome, but Cagliares soon brought its revocation on the excuse that the palace would only serve as an ordinary residence of the bishop and, in case of siege, as a place of refuge for his canons.

Vasconcellos died on 7 March 1623.

ANTOINE DE PAULE
1623-1636

*O*n the accession of Antoine de Paule, a knight of French nationality who became grand master on 10 March 1623, the Maltese hoped for a reform of government. But their ardent expectations were doomed to disappointment.

The new grand master succeeded in maintaining the high standard which the navy of the island had attained under his predecessor. With the assistance of the engineer Floriani da Macerata, he began the extension of the outer fortifications of Floriana. Lack of funds, however, did not permit him to complete them.

The same year that de Paule was elected head of the Order, Pope Urban VIII succeeded to the pontificate. The new pontiff, who was not friendly towards the new grand master, instituted at Rome a permanent congregation presided over by a cardinal to control the affairs of Malta. This body, acting as if invested with absolute authority, began to dispose of the Italian commendaries without regard to the prerogatives of the grand master. Pope Urban substituted the title of Most Serene Highness with that of Eminence and relieved knights of the right to dispose of their possessions by will.

The king of Spain tried to intervene with the pope in order to induce him to dissolve the above-mentioned congregation. The grand master and the council also sent Monsignor Imbroll, prior of the conventual church, a man of great ability and long-tried prudence, to argue their case. Through his efforts, the powers of the congregation were considerably restricted thus reconciling both the Order and the pope.

In 1625 the tribunal of the *Fabbrica di San Pietro* was instituted to deal with pious bequests. The bishop fruitlessly resisted this encroachment upon his jurisdiction, but at length the unbecoming conflicts of authority between the tribunal and the episcopal court induced Pope Alexander VII to suppress the tribunal and grant its powers to the Inquisition.

In 1632 the grand master ordered a census of the islands to be taken. At least three figures were taken showing a population numbering 54,463 inhabitants; another, 51,750; and a third, 41,750.

No events of striking importance occurred during the last years of de Paule's life which ended on 9 June 1636.

JEAN-PAUL LASCARIS CASTELLAR
1636-1657

*O*n 13 June 1636 Jean-Paul Lascaris Castellar, a knight of Provence, became grand master.

At the time of the election of Lascaris, the viceroy of Sicily refused the export of more than the ordinary quantity of grain, and the grand master appealed to the viceroy of Naples. When war broke out between Spain and France, some French knights accepted the command of armed vessels from their sovereign. The court of Spain, taking taking exception to this, refused food supplies and confiscated the money which the French knights had in Sicily.

Notwithstanding these hard times, the work of Floriani, suspended under the preceding grand master, was again taken at hand. Under the direction of Fr Vincenzo Maculano, Santa Margherita hill was fortified, the mole of Valletta was enlarged, the Lazzaretto was constructed, the Public Library was established, and other public works were undertaken. All this entailed imposing new taxes.

The army was also reorganized. This, however, led to problems with the bishop, who ordained an excessive number of both married and unmarried clerics, who were exempted from military service. Lascaris had to appeal to both the king of Spain and Pope Urban VIII before married clerics were declared subject to military service.

Lascaris would have been more popular had he not, like some of his predecessors, laid hands upon the rights of the communes. The two constitutional municipalities of Valletta and Notabile were put under the presidency of the same seneschal who would alternate meetings between them.

In 1640 Lascaris promulgated a body of laws which, according to the confused method of that time, dealt indiscriminately with matters pertaining to domestic public law, civil law, criminal law, procedure, and police. On 25 May 1644 he introduced printing and giving licence to Pompeo del Fiore for a printing press. He also prohibited for ten years the importation of certain books under a pecuniary penalty together with the confiscation of the books themselves.

He died on 14 August 1657.

MARTIN DE REDIN
1657-1660

*T*hree days after the death of de Lascaris, Martin de Redin, an Aragonese, then viceroy of Sicily, was proclaimed grand master. He assumed the government of the island on 10 September. His election was marked by an insiduous campaign against him by a party of senior knights supported by Inquisitor Odi. The pope approved his election and Odi, who had falsely accused de Redin of malpractice, was recalled to Rome and replaced by Mgr. Casanati.

Commander de Mandolx was again appointed general of the galleys. He, immediately, set sail to join the pope's squadron in Sicily. On his way, near Augusta he met two Muslim brigantines which he charged and captured. With the pope's ships he later set sail for Constantinople. In the meantime the two squadrons chased three Muslim vessels, two of which were captured. Later, they again steered westwards and made for their respective ports.

Apart of this incident, De Redin's brief term of office passed by without any notable military or naval operations, without any alarms of hostile invasion, and without any dearth of provisions. So abundant, in fact, was the supply of corn that it was found necessary to construct new granaries.

One of the first thoughts of de Redin was to provide for the defence of the coast. Until then guard on the coasts at night was provided by Maltese enlisted in the angara. This was chiefly done for the purpose of hindering the landing of the enemy. However, it was only indifferently kept as countrymen were already worn out with the fatigue of the day. To remedy this very serious inconvenience, he caused thirteen towers to be built along the coast in less than a year, arming each with two guns and maintaining in each a small garrison of paid guards.

At the beginning of 1660, the war between Spain and France ended; its termination relieved the Order of the great difficulty experienced in observing the strict neutrality it had declared. But the worthy de Redin was not destined to enjoy the benefits of peace for long.

He died on 6 February of the same year.

ANNET DE CLERMONT
DE CHATTES GESSAN
1660

*A*nnet de Clermont de Chattes Gessan of the langue of Auvergne was bailiff of Lyon when he was elected grand master on 6 February 1660. His election, secured solely on his own merits, was acknowledged two days after thus making him sovereign prince of Malta and Gozo.

The title of sovereign was enjoyed by the Clermont family since the time the lands of Dauphiny and Savoy were the Clermont's possession before 1340. The viscounts of Clermont family had then levied troops, made alliances and treaties with other aristocratic families, and waged wars whenever their interests or security was threatened. Because of this they had the right to impose taxes on their subjects to make adequate preparations for emergencies. Their castles of Chavacert and Saussin upon the river Guè were consequently always garrisoned by the best men and thus made their estates impregnable.

During the few months in government, Grand Master de Clermont did not show his family's talents. His measures were good but strong and, though well adapted to the climate of peace then reigning between France and Spain, were also aimed to safeguard Malta's neutrality against the arrogance of alien men-of-war. Mercantile activity in Malta's ports thus increased bringing riches and benevolence from all Christian States.

Annet de Clermont was a man of great courage and this, together with his piety and zeal for religion, made him humane and popular both with the knights and the populace. He would probably have become a successful and popular grand master. Providence, however, disposed otherwise. A serious wound which he received during the siege of Mahometa kept bleeding until his health detoriated.

De Clermont died on the arms of his spiritual directors and surrounded by his beloved knights on 2 June 1660, aged 73.

RAPHAEL COTONER
1660-1663

*R*aphael Cotoner, bailiff of Majorca, was elected grand master on 5 June 1660.

At that time the war with the Turks over Candia was at its peak. The Venetians were continually asking for help from all Christian princes of Europe. Malta responded generously and, with the blessings of Pope Alexander VII, Grand Master Cotoner sent his fleet to help in the reconquest of lost islands. The Maltese put up a good show. They succeeded in routing the enemy at several strategic points and in capturing the towns of Calogero and Calami.

The fleet also proved its worth on other occasions. On 24 January it attacked a Tunisian vessel off Capo Passero and carried away some 130 slaves amongst whom were the son of the bey of Tunis and a choaux of the sultan of Turkey.

In spite of the Order's expenses in the war of Candia, Raphael Cotoner did not sacrifice the more important projects at home. His good administration, in fact, managed to cope both with his generosity as an ally of the Venetians in war and his magnificence in his role as prince of the Maltese islands. Malta had rarely had a better time. Disputes with the bishop and the inquisitor were few and relationship with the Maltese excellent. He is best remembered for the improvement of the infirmary. The new ward, 520 ft long, was believed to be the largest in Europe. Hygenic conditions at the infirmary were improved. These included the introduction of single beds to replace the traditional treble-patient ones then still in use all over the continent.

Raphael Cotoner was also a great patron of the arts. He was responsible for bringing to the island the Calabrian painter, Mattia Preti, and entrusting him with the painting of St John's. Unfortunately, he did not live long enough to see it.

He contacted the fever which at the time was ravaging the island and he died on 20 October 1663.

NICHOLAS COTONER
1663-1680

Nicholas Cotoner, brother of the preceding grand master and a man of rigid and austere temper, was wanted by none and was elected by all, as he himself said. During his term of office, which began on 23 October, he pleased few, disgusted many, and enjoyed the flattery rather than the love of those around him. But he was bold in his designs. The semi-circular fortifications around the Three Cities are named Cottonera after him. Besides this great and arduous work, which was carried out under the direction of the engineer Valperga sent to him by the duke of Savoy, he added considerably to the works begun by Floriani and Maculano. He levelled the quay of the Grand Harbour and he instituted the school of anatomy and surgery.

To meet the expenses entailed by these works he levied, with the consent of Clement X, a tax upon landed property, including also that of the Church. Although consequently suspended, this tax was replaced by duties on coffee, brandy, soap, coral, tobacco, and playing cards.

During this period Fort Ricasoli was constructed, also from plans by Valperga. The new fort received its name from Bailiff Francesco Ricasoli, who donated 30,000 crowns for the work, and devoted a further 3,000 out of his annual income to the same purpose.

The islands were not disturbed by wars or by fighting under Cotoner, but the galleys of the Order, together with 500 Maltese soldiers and 80 knights, assisted the enterprise of Louis XIV of France, challenging the Barbary corsairs who were trying to establish a colony upon the coast of Algeria. He also helped construct a fort and harbour for the protection of French vessels. The grand master also assisted the Venetians with 400 Maltese soldiers and 62 knights in their war with the Turks in Candia (Crete); and he afforded English war-vessels the use and protection of the Malta harbour in their operations against Tripoli.

A pestilence, which broke out towards the end of 1675, caused a loss of 11,000 lives in six months.

Nicholas Cotoner felt the necessity of a radical reform in legislation, and appointed a commission for this purpose. But he died on 29 April 1680 before the work was completed.

GREGORIO CARAFA DE ROCCELLA
1680-1690

Gregorio Carafa, prior of La Roccella, was elected head of the Order on 2 May 1680. Carafa's accession come in the course of a fierce war between the Turks and the Austrians. Although Malta was not directly involved, the great assistance given by Maltese ships in their frequent skirmishes with Muslim shipping in the Levant was greatly appreciated by Emperor Leopold. Their actions indeed proved that the Order's fleet still ranked high among the maritime powers of the Mediterranean.

Among Carafa's early projects were those of the fortifications initiated by his predecessor. With the advice of his council, he secured the service of G. Grunemberg, who was perhaps the most experienced military engineer in Sicily. With his plans and under his supervision the forts of St Elmo and St Angelo were modernized.

The statutes of Carafa, promulgated on 12 September 1680, with a want of method attributable more to the period of their compilation than to their compiler, dealt with the rights and the duties of public officials, contracts, the commoner forms of crime, the forms of judicial proceedings, and some matters relating to police.

In 1684 the Order joined the alliance that had been formed between Austria, Poland, and Venice against the Turks, furnishing galleys, 900 soldiers, and 100 knights for the capture of the Morea. Three years afterwards the Maltese fought bravely at Castelnuovo. A year later a British squadron, consisting of 7 ships, commanded by the duke of Groftin, the son of Charles II, was given a warm welcome when it entered the Grand Harbour. A misunderstanding in protocol between the prince duke and the grand master spoilt what would otherwise have been the resumption of an excellent relationship

and which might have led to the reopening of the English langue. This unfortunate incident was made even worse by the sad news that the confederate fleets attempting the blockade of Negroponte had been defeated after losing the better part of their forces, including 400 Maltese and 26 knights who fell victim to the plague.

Seized with a violent fever, Carafa ended his days on 21 July 1690, lamented by the people to whom he had particularly endeared himself by his affable manners.

ADRIEN DE WIGNACOURT
1690-1697

*A*drien de Wignacourt, grand treasurer of the Order and nephew of the Grand Master Alof de Wignacourt (1601-22), was elected grand master on 24 July 1690. He celebrated the beginning of his rule with an act of munificence. He gave a pension to the widows and orphans of the Maltese who fell in the service of the Order during his predecessor's term of office. He also ordered the maintenance of a galliot to police the sea around Malta and to clear them of Barbary corsairs.

On 12 January 1693 a series of earthquakes hit the south-eastern part of Sicily. Catania and Augusta were then almost totally razed to the ground leaving tens of thousands of dead beneath the rubble. Some parts of Malta and Gozo were also slightly affected. Damage was done to the steeple of the Romanesque cathedral in Malta, to the *Matrice*, and to parish church of St George in Gozo. He ordered Chev. Ferrao to reconstruct the Order's oven in Augusta and entrusted the French military engineer, Chev. Vendôsme, to assess the extent of the damage in Malta.

Adrien de Wignacourt refitted the ships of the Order's fleet with the necessary masts and sails in order to make every craft sea-worthy and also built an arsenal for the construction of galleys and new magazines for the storage of war munitions.

The state of the treasury at this time was such as to permit the expenditure of considerable sums upon works of public utility and in acts of beneficence. This was made particularly possible through the personal intervention of Pope Innocent XII who, as a former inquisitor of Malta, was well acquainted with the islands' needs. Besides exempting the possessions of the Order from a tax to which his monarchs wished to subject them, the pope further induced the king of France and the duke of Savoy to refrain from levying any

contribution whatsoever upon the same possession. To make good the lack of hands at the galleys, he also sent the grand master a large number of convicts who offered to serve as rowers upon the galleys. Finally, by reconciling the Order with Genoa, he procured new sources of refilling the Order's coffers and thus provided the knights with the much needed finances.

Adrien de Wignacourt died on 4 February 1697.

RAMON PERELLOS Y ROCCAFUL
1697-1720

*R*amon Perellos, an Aragonese, on becoming grand master on 7 February 1697, also attacked the rights and prerogatives of the *Università*. In addition to the seneschal, who was already president of the *Consiglio Popolare*, he also appointed one of the *uditori* as a member of that body; the *uditori* were the grand master's chief ministers in all that related to the maintenance of his jurisdiction and the administration of justice.

Perellos, however, is credited with having assisted the development and growth of culture and commerce. He built large stone warehouses and introduced the mercantile laws which he promulgated on 4 September 1697 as the *Consolato del Mare*. He obtained permission to start the ship-of-the-line squadron from Pope Innocent XII, who was always well disposed towards the Order. The pope restituted the commanderies, which other pontiffs had always disposed of, and he secured an abundance of corn for the island.

The jurisdictional conflicts between bishop, inquisitor, and grand master became still more lively under his rule, and, at times, more noisy and disorderly in character. However, Innocent, again exercising his friendly offices, managed to contain all differences which divided them, giving fair consideration to the rights of one and all.

Perellos is, perhaps, best remembered for his generosity towards the embellishment of the conventual church of St John's. As part of his *gioia* he secured from the famous Gobelin factory in France a set of 12 artistic tapestries by the Flemish master Judocus de Vos representing episodes from the life of Christ and the missionary call of the Church. They were woven to the designs of world-famous artists such as Peter Paul Rubens. He also paid for the monumental statue of *The Baptism of Christ* by Giuseppe Mazzuoli in St John's. Another set of 10

tapestries representing beasts and exotic plants, also paid from his own pocket, were woven for the Magistral Palace in Valletta. He also built Porte des Bombes.

Infirm of mind during the last three years of his life, Perellos breathed his last on 10 January 1720.

MARCANTONIO ZONDADARI
1720-1722

$\mathcal{M}$arc'Antonio Zondadari, a noble from Siena belonging to the langue of Italy, became grand master on 13 January 1720. Unlike his predecessor, he was not very much in favour of Spain which still claimed its rights on Malta. However, he kept the Order's good relationship with the Spanish authorities. As was customary, on his installation ceremony, he sent the falcon to the viceroy of Sicily which had then just passed into Habsburg hands, thus ensuring an excellent politico-economic climate in which commerce between Malta and Sicily could prosper.

The correctness of Zondadari was almost religious, even towards the Maltese. It is said that because of the ambiguous relations of the Order with the Maltese, Zondadari refused to take the oath to observe the rights and privileges of the *Università*. The story is described by the Order's chroniclers as being unfounded. But other historians believed that Zondadari's behaviour originated from his knowledge that at the time of his succession the Maltese had been left with no rights and privileges.

Consequently, soon after patching his political quarrels with Spain and the new Habsburg rulers in Sicily, Zondadari turned his attention to domestic problems. He showed his trust in the *Università* by giving them a seat of office in Valletta, where the prices of bread and other commodities were fixed every day; invested the jurats with ceremonial privileges; entrusted them with the administration of the *Monte delle Fortificazioni*; and allowed the *Università* to raise taxes on wine, meat, and consumables and to administer their proceeds according to their needs.

He also re-organized the fleet of the Order, fostered mercantile in lieu of corsairing activity, and declared Malta's harbour a free port (*scala* Frà *nca*) to all Christian shipping. In Gozo he reinforced the fortifications and increased the provisions.

Zondadari proved his worth by maintaining a balanced economy which left the Order's treasury in a healthy state when he died on 16 June 1722.

ANTONIO MANOEL DE VILHENA
1722-1736

*A*ntonio Manoel de Vilhena, a Portuguese of the langue of Castille, succeeded Zondadari on 19 June 1722. His noble birth and personal qualities were coupled to his wisdom and knowledge of the Order's regulations. He gradually rose to prominence through diligence and hard work. He, in fact, had hardly finished his caravans when he was made captain of the admiral's galley. He was twice wounded in engagements with Muslim ships. He was later made major and then colonel of the militia, cross of grace in 1696, commissioner of the navy in 1698, commissioner of war in 1701, and grand chancellor in 1713.

On Manoel's rise to the magistracy, the political horizon became for a time overcast by a Turkish plot to capture Malta. The grand master, warned in time, put his defences in order and preserved the island from attack. Although the Turkish squadron duly appeared, Admiral Abdi, who commanded it, fired a few shots and threatened Manoel with the most terrible consequences if he did not set free all his Muslim slaves. The grand master replied that he was ready to treat with a view of exchanging slaves. The Porte not only accepted the proposal but wished to conclude a treaty of peace with the Order. The proposed treaty was, however, strongly opposed by the chief officers of the sultan's navy.

The grand master also modernized the island's fortifications. He built a fort upon Lazaretto island in Marsamxett, remodelled the entrance to Mdina, and founded the suburb of Floriana. There, he instituted a home for poor unmarried women and another one for incurables. He also built a theatre in Valletta. He recodified Malta's laws making them mainly concerned on matters of internal public law, civil law, mercantile law, criminal law, judicial law, and the police. He also reformed the Order's statutes in 1723. Manoel reduced the customs duties, provided funds for public works, and ensured an abundance of provisions at low prices.

Grand Master Manoel de Vilhena breathed his last on 12 December 1736, having gained the affections and the esteem of the Maltese.

RAIMONDO DESPUIG
1736-1741

*O*n 16 December 1736 Raymond Despuig, bailiff of Majorca, from the priory of Catalonia and a man of conspicuous probity, was elected grand master. He was the nephew of the Grand Masters Raphael and Nicolas Cotoner, being the son of their sister.

During the four years of his magistracy, Despuig experienced relative peace and stability originating from the long period of peace between the Christian and Muslim States. Taking advantage of such peaceful conditions, he spent most of his time trying to settle thorny affairs within the internal administration of his Order.

His efforts were, however, somewhat frustrated when, on 6 February 1740, Pope Clement XII died and, because of the long conclave which lasted until 16 August, all progress came to a standstill. When Cardinal Prospero Lambertini of Bologna, who was a friend of Malta, was elected pontiff, the Order received added privileges for which other countries became jealous. Benedict XIV, as the new pope chose to be called, was ever ready to help the Maltese. Despuig, however, was then feeling too old for his job.

Weighed down with years, sickly, and destined not to enjoy his position for long, Despuig made no administrative or legislative reform. Instead, he was able to rid the seas of the Levant of the corsairs that infested them. He regulated precedence among families according to the title of each. He withdrew the silver coinage of his predecessors and re-issued new one in debased weights.

In spite of his old age Despuig did not abandon the excellent works of reconstruction initiated by his predecessor. In 1739 he built Mondion's new gate at Mdina, moving it some 3 *canne* (about 7 metres) to the left of the old one. A bridge was also built to provide a new gateway to the imposing entrance. The old entrance, still visible in the ditch on the right-hand side of the bridge, was later barred with masonry from the breach made for the gate.

Raymond Despuig, whose magistracy was marked by various works of piety, died on 15 January 1741.

EMANUEL PINTO DE FONSECA
1741-1773

*D*espuig was succeeded on 18 January 1741 by Emanuel Pinto de Fonseca, a Portuguese who had lived in Malta from his childhood and who was considered by the Maltese more as a compatriot than as a foreigner. He could, in fact, also speak their own language.

Combining the title of 'Highness' conferred on the grand masters by Ferdinand II with that of 'Eminence' granted by Pope Urban VIII, Pinto assumed the title of 'Most Eminent Highness' and called himself 'Prince of Malta'. No sovereign objected to these titles. But Charles Bourbon, king of Naples, wished to reaffirm his rights of sovereignty over Malta and Gozo according to the Act of Cession of 24 March 1530. Pinto disputed such claims and in the ensuing quarrel commerce was disrupted and the commanderies of the Order in the Two Sicilies were sequestrated. The timely intervention of Pope Benedict XIV brought relations back to normal.

The favourable outcome of the quarrel added further to Pinto's prestige among the monarchs of Europe. He, in turn, reciprocated the respect and was even ready to accept the international rules of good relationship among nations. As a consequence the influence of France over the Order grew and prospects of an opening towards the Levant seemed brighter. In fact, Pinto prevented the fleet of the Order from engaging in any corsairing enterprises against Muslim shipping.

Pinto's magistracy was not without internal incidents. In 1749 Mustapha Pasha of Rhodes, who was in Malta as captive of the knights, plotted to kill the grand master and seize Malta on behalf of the sultan of Turkey. Fortunately, the plot was discovered and 38 of the conspirators were put to death.

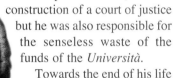

Mustapha, strong in the protection of France, escaped the fury of the people and was allowed to go free.

Pinto will be remembered most for his enlightened despotism. He set up the university of studies, made many defensive and useful public works, and the construction of a court of justice but he was also responsible for the senseless waste of the funds of the *Università*.

Towards the end of his life Pinto rendered himself so hated that neither the knights nor the people lamented his death which took place on 23 January 1773.

FRANCISCO XIMENES DE TEXADA
1773-1775

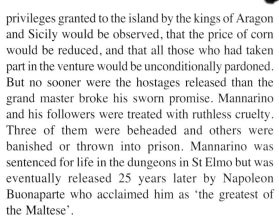

*T*he most popular candidate for the magistracy was Francisco Ximenes of the langue of Aragon from whom a liberal reform in the State administration was expected. He was elected on 28 January 1773, but all illusions and expectations of progress were very soon dispelled by his autocratic and tyrannical policies. He suppressed many offices, reduced salaries, imposed limitations upon the pursuit of game, and increased the price of corn, thus occassioning much misery. He governed with extreme rigour and treated those who had served him well with haughtiness and ingratitude.

Already during the time of his detested predecessor, dissension among the Maltese was rife. A movement had been formed to reform the government by force and to secure the observance of the rights and prerogatives of the *Università*. In 1772 dissension was somewhat eased following interventions by Dun Gejt Mannarino, a young priest who had built high hopes that Ximenes could in time bring about the much-needed reform. But, as month after month passed, Mannarino's hopes proved illusory.

In an effort to play a decisive blow at the government, Mannarino persuaded other leaders of the people that only an armed intervention could bring Ximenes to his senses. A small group of Maltese, both secular and clerical, joined him and thus broke out the most ill-considered of rebellions, known as 'the rising of the priests'.

On the night of 8 September 1775 a joint surprise attack was made on St James Cavalier and Fort St Elmo. The following morning at daybreak, for the first time in Malta's history, the Maltese colours, then a red flag with the effigy of St Paul in it, flew on the walls of Malta's strongest bastions. For several days Mannarino kept St Elmo's captain and guards as hostages until finally it was agreed that the privileges granted to the island by the kings of Aragon and Sicily would be observed, that the price of corn would be reduced, and that all those who had taken part in the venture would be unconditionally pardoned. But no sooner were the hostages released than the grand master broke his sworn promise. Mannarino and his followers were treated with ruthless cruelty. Three of them were beheaded and others were banished or thrown into prison. Mannarino was sentenced for life in the dungeons in St Elmo but was eventually released 25 years later by Napoleon Buonaparte who acclaimed him as 'the greatest of the Maltese'.

A decree issued the same day declared, that the grand master and the Order had never violated the rights of the Maltese, that the price of corn was not raised without the sanction of the jurats of the *università* and that the terms given for the surrender of Fort St Elmo were honoured.

Ximenes died of a sudden illness on 9 November 1775, thus closing two years of unequalled shame.

EMANUEL DE ROHAN POLDUC
1775-1797

*T*he Bailiff Emmanuel de Rohan, a Frenchman, was elected grand master on 12 November 1775.

De Rohan began his reign with acts of clemency and kindness, setting free political prisoners and treasury debtors, recalling and pardoning galley deserters, and donating considerable sums of money in charity. He endeavoured at the same time to lessen the great division between the knights and the Maltese, a state of affairs which had always been a source of very grave annoyance. He limited the right of immunity of certain wayside chapels and confirmed the institution of the university.

De Rohan owes his place in history chiefly to the code of laws which bears his name. In respect of civil rights, it marks a real milestone in the history of legislation in Malta. In fact, it took into consideration local customs and traditions and included improve- ments made in Italy and France in legal enactments and procedures.

The last years of de Rohan's long term of office were very different from the first. The suppression of the Order in France in September 1792 and the outbreak of war in nearly all the countries where it had possessions almost bankrupted the treasury.

The Order was obliged to look for heavy loans in Malta and abroad. In 1796, unable to borrow further, it was compelled to melt for minting purposes the silver plates from its ships and galleys, a part of the personal dinner service of the grand master, and a part of its silverware including the hospital utensils. Lack of food began to be felt in the island, commerce declined, and new industrial projects ended in failure.

The Order felt it necessary to cultivate friendship with other nations. In 1793 and 1794, by public acts under the seal of the castellan, the grand master favoured the enrolment of Maltese for service on English warships. He threatened to punish deserters with three years' enforced service on the galleys and also gave judges summary powers to condemn them.

The fear of losing its Polish possessions, then yielding 120,000 florins annually, induced the Order to make friendly overtures to Russia. Catherine II assured the grand master that the Order would not be deprived of its possessions, and Paul I, who succeeded her, confirmed his mother's dispositions and promised 180,000 florins, a sum which he afterwards increased for the setting up of the grand priory of Russia.

These dealings with schismatic Russia gave umbrage to France and Spain and, far from saving the Order, tended to hasten its fall. De Rohan, foreseeing the Order's end rapidly approaching, said on his death bed: 'I am, at any rate, the last grand master, at least, of an Order, illustrious and independent.' With these words, he passed away on 13 July 1797.

FERDINAND VON HOMPESCH
1797-1798

*I*n the midst of impending calamity, on 17 July 1797, Ferdinand von Hompesch became grand master, the last of the feudatories of Charles V.

Hompesch had come to Malta as a young page to Grand Master Pinto. Rapidly attaining the dignity of grand cross, he was for 25 years the representative of the Order at the court of Vienna and he returned to the island as head of the langue of Bavaria. Upright, frank, and affable in manner, he was beloved by the people who rejoiced at his accession. But he had neither the capability nor the firmness which the times required.

Hompesch published a number of laws, most of them relating to local security matters. So long as he was well-counselled, he appointed men of repute to positions of trust, but when he acted on his own he proved himself weak and incompetent.

Meantime, things went from bad to worse. Commerce and industry steadily declined, salaries went in arrears, vacant situations were left unfilled, and food became scarce, thus increasing the misery and discontent of the country.

Napoleon Buonaparte, then wishing to make the Mediterranean a French lake, was planning to lay hands on the island. Setting out from Toulon upon his proposed Egyptian expedition, he appeared off Malta on 9 June 1798 and demanded permission to enter the harbour with his ships to water. The council of the Order considering that Malta was a neutral port could not access to the demand of the French leader. Instead it consented to allow only four vessels at a time. The French disregarded the Order's offer, and next day their troops landed at various points in Malta and Gozo.

The islands were not prepared for war and after a feeble resistance they offered to surrender. A deputation of the principal citizens went on the French ship *L'Orient* where Napoleon held his council of war and after some hours of negotiations signed the terms of capitulation.

The surrender of the islands was received with mixed feelings. The country people were not happy, but not the inhabitants of the cities, who recognized that the Order could not continue its useless existence much longer, were glad to rid themselves of the despotism of the knights.

After ratifying the capitulation, Hompesch set out for Trieste on 18 June. He abdicated on 6 July 1799 and retired to Montpellier where he died on 12 May 1805.

THE ORDER AFTER MALTA

View of Valletta with the Order's fleet leaving the Grand Harbour

After his expulsion from Malta, Grand Master Hompesch, together with other faithful members of the Order, sailed to Trieste where they were given hospitality by the emperor of Austria. On his arrival he publicly condemned both the French aggression in Malta and the disloyal behaviour of knights who had either joined the French in Malta or went to Russia where they plotted with Tsar Paul I to depose him.

The desperate situation in which the Order of St John found itself following its expulsion from Malta made its existence critical. On one hand there were fears that with the isolation of its grand master and the consequent loss of most of its revenues, the Order could gradually loose its identity and be dissolved; on the other, there were hopes of rescue and revival under the powerful protectorship of Tsar Paul who, though schismatic, had offered the Order a home and financial security.

In recognition of such help, a group of knights in St Petersburg met in council in 1798 and elected Paul I grand master before Hompesch had even resigned. When Paul died on 24 March 1801, the political situation then prevailing in Europe made it impossible for the chapter general to meet to elect a new grand master. The sovereign council, which Paul had set up to safeguard the sovereignty and prerogatives of the Order, consequently asked the pope to choose the new grand master from a list of knights nominated by the Order's priories. On 9 February 1803 the pope chose Bailiff Giovanni Tommasi as the Order's grand master.

Tommasi had high hopes that Malta would be restored to the Order once the English pulled out of the island. Sir Alexander Ball had been sent to the island as minister plenipotentiary for the Order.

With this hope in view, the new grand master first set up his headquarters in Messina and later in Catania, where he waited until the belligerent states abided by the Treaty of Amiens. Article X of this Treaty had established that Malta would be returned to the knights on condition that the two langues of England and France be dissolved and that a new Maltese langue instituted.

The Order was contrary to any external interference and the imposition of new articles in its statute could not be approved without the consent of a general chapter. Besides, because of its aristocratic nature, it could not accept the Maltese as an autonomous langue. Russia, in particular, was averse to its inclusion.

Hopes of an early settlement continued to fade out when, on 30 May 1803, hostilities between Britain and France were resumed. By that time the British had already made up their mind not to leave the island and, with the pretext that the Maltese were contrary to the Order's return and that they wanted the British monarch to protect them, they instructed Capt. Alexander Ball, whom they had originally sent as minister plenipotentiary to the Order, to assume the post of civil commissioner and to order all alien troops out of the island.

Grand Master Giovanni Battista Tommasi (1803-05)

Grand Master Tsar Paul I (1799-1802)

In the meantime Alexander I, who succeeded his father Paul as tsar of Russia, refused the magistracy and returned the magisterial regalia together with other documents to the Order. In the meantime Pope Pius VII with a brief of 11 September 1801 nominated bailiff Bartolomeo Respoli as grand master. But Respoli turned down the offer and in cosequence, the Bailiff Caracciolo di San Ermano and after him Commendatore Romagnoso were offered the lieutenancy of the magistary but these also refused to accept the office. Finally, Frà Giovanni Battista Tommasi was chosen as grand master on 9 February 1803. The sovereign council, which was originally set up by Tsar Paul I, also accepted the authority of the new grand master and soon after announced its own dissolution. A new sovereign council was consequently formed and assembled in Messina to organize the future of the Order.

On 13 June 1805 Grand Master Tommasi died at Catania. No successor was afterwards elected for 70 years. This was a period of great difficulty for the Order. With the three langues of France already suppressed in 1792, the priories of Italy confiscated between 1798 and 1800, and the langues of Spain incorporated within the Spanish crown in 1801, the Order could hardly survive. The few surviving knights were scattered throughout Europe. To add insult to injury splinter groups mushroomed wherever a langue had previously existed, some of non-Catholic denomination, thus usurping in their own way the Order's identity.

The lack of a proper home disrupted the role of the Order as shield of Christendom and nurse of the sick and the poor. For 24 years after, it roamed about the cities of Italy in search of hospitality. It stayed for 22 years in Catania. Then, in 1826, it moved to Ferrara and, a few years later, to Rome.

In the meantime it was ruled by a series of nine lieutenants, who were elected by knights and ratified by the pope. These were:

Grand Master Galeazzo Von Thun und Hohenstein (1905-31)

Innico Guevara Suardo	1805-14
Andrea di Giovanni	1814-21
Antonio Busca	1821-83
Carlo Candida	1834-45
Filippo di Colleredo-Mels	1845-64
Alessandro Borgia	1865-71
Giov. Franc. Ceschi a Santa Croce	1871-79

This was a time of reconstruction. By 1839 the langues of Italy, Spain, and Germany were reconstructed and in 1854 Pope Pius IX approved the new statutes. On 28 March 1879 Pope Leo XIII, who had been on Peter's throne for a year, appointed Lieutenant Giovanni Francesco Ceschi a Santa Croce as grand master. He was soon recognized by various sovereigns and heads of state and thus took right of precedence over all other chivalrous Orders. The new grand master's main task was to re-organize the administration of the Order restoring its original role of a hospitable association.

Grand Master Giovanni Battista Ceschi a Santa Croce (1879-1905)

Grand Master Ludovico Chigi della Rovere Albani (1931-51)

Beside the hospital at Naples, the polyclinic for child invalids at Milan, and St John's dispensary at Montmarte in Paris where hundreds of poor were looked after and fed everyday, Grand Master Ceschi also opened a hospice at Tantur in Jerusalem. In Italy he also organized an association of Italian knights to look after the wounded and the sanitary service on the battlefronts. These were assisted by the service of three ambulance trains with 200 beds in each, a mobile clinic, and a camp-hospital. This initiative was imitated by the German langue, which through the good services of the priory of Bohemian and the associations of Wesphalia and Silesia built hospitals in Treblinz, Ribnik, Kuzendorf, Breslavia, Friedland, and Schurgast.

When Grand Master Ceschi died in 1905 the Order was no more 'an obsolete medieval association of warring aristocratic knights'. It was a reformed Order of hospitallers, full of care for others, and ready to provide medical assistance wherever it was required.

Frà Galeazzo Von Thun und Hohenstein, who succeeded Ceschi in 1905, possessed the same pious character as his predecessor. He continued with the previous humanitarian projects in time of war and peace until he died in 1931. Among the works of charity for which Thun will be most remembered is the institution of leprosaria which he set up in various parts of Africa.

Thun was succeeded by Frà Ludovico Chigi della Rovere Albani in 1931. In spite of the difficult times in which Europe was then passing, the new grand master intensified the Order's humanitarian activities wherever he saw it necessary. These activities were not suspended during World War II and the Order's aeroplanes and ambulances, marked with the eight-

Grand Master Angelo de Mojana (1962-88)

pointed cross, continued to convey assistance to the sick and the poor both on the battlefields of Europe and in distant hamlets of developing countries, like Eritrea, Sudan, Nigeria, and Congo. Mercy missions were also sent to places of national disaster as the 1910 earthquake of Messina and the frequent floods in South America.

On the death of Chigi Albani della Rovere in 1951, the Order found itself at loggerheads with members of the Church authorities in Rome over its re-organization and was, thus, again placed under the rule of a lieutenant of the grand master. Between 1951 and 1955 it was ruled by Frà Antonio Hercolani and, between 1955 and 1962, by Frà Ernesto Paternò Castello. In 1961 the knights, assembled in Rome in a 'complete council of state', elected Frà Angelo de Mojana di Cologna as the new grand master. Soon after his election he convened a chapter general to re-organize the Order and modernize its institution.

The new constitution of the Order kept the grand master as its head but it envisaged the establishment of a sovereign council whose members, elected by the general chapter, were to advise the grand master. This brought the Order under the rule of chancery, chaired by the grand chancellor who was elected by the chapter general. It also had to have a judicial council and a board of auditors.

The old priories, which in medieval times had been regarded as 'types of convents housing knights of a particular language' forming part of the organization of a langue were retained. So also were the sub-priories and the grand priories. New ones, however, were created for the same purpose but were known by a more modern name of 'national associations'. These also kept their old aims but in a way which conformed with the laws of the country to which they belonged.

In Malta the Maltese Association of the Sovereign Military Order of Malta was formally set up in 1965. It has its headquarters in Valletta next to the church of Our Lady of Victories. Its first president was His Grace the Archbishop Mgr. Sir Michael Gonzi. He was succeeded by Chev. Roger de Giorgio. On the latter's retirement in 1999, the members of the Association elected Chev. Dr Philip Attard Montalto, LL.D.

Grand Master Andrew Bertie (1988-)

The Maltese Association also set up a blood-bank run jointly with the Church and State and a clinic for diabetics.

Since the institution of the Maltese Association two grand masters have paid an official visit to the island: the first by Frà Angelo de Mojana in 1962 while the second by Frà Andrew Bertie in 1989. In 1999 the Order also acquired Fort St Angelo on temporary lease for 99 years.

The Order enjoys diplomatic relations by means of accredited representatives with a number of countries all over the globe. These include the Holy See, Malta, Italy, Portugal, Spain, Argentina, and Brazil. It also maintains official delegations in Belgium, Germany, France, Monaco, and Switzerland. It is also represented in several international organizations amongst which the United Nations, where it has observer status, the Council of Europe, and UNESCO.

LIST OF THE GRAND MASTERS

1. Blessed Gèrard, founder	f 3 Sept. 1120	
2. Blessed Raymond du Puy	1120-58/60	
3. Auger de Balben	1158/60-62/3	
4. Arnaud de Comps	1162/3	
5. Gilbert d'Assailly	1163-69/70	
6. Gaston de Murols	c.1170-c.72	
7. Joubert	c. 1172-77	
8. Roger des Moulins	1177-87	
9. Ermengard d'Asp	1188-c.90	
10. Garnier de Naplous	1189/90-92	
11. Geoffroy de Donjon	1193-1202	
12. Alphonse de Portugal	1202-06	
13. Geoffroy Le Rat	1206-07	
14. Garin de Montaigu	1207-27/8	
15. Bertrand de Thessy	1228-c.31	
16. Guèrin	c.1231-36	
17. Bertrand de Comps	1236-39/40	
18. Pierre de Vieille-Bride	1239/40-42	
19. Guillaume de Châteauneuf	1242-58	
20. Hugues de Revel	1258-77	
21. Nicolas Lorgne	1277/8-84	
22. Jean de Villiers	1284/5-93/4	
23. Odon de Pins	1294-96	
24. Guillaume de Villaret	1296-1305	
25. Foulques de Villaret	1305-19	
26. Hèlion de Villenueve	1319-46	
27. Dieudonne de Gozon	1346-53	
28. Pierre de Corneillan	1353-55	
29. Roger de Pins	1355-65	
30. Raymond Bèrenger	1365-74	
31. Robert de Juilliac	1374-76	
32. Jean Fernandez de Heredia	1376-96	
33. Richard Caracciolo	1383-95	
34. Philibert de Naillac	1396-1421	
35. Antoine Fluvian de la Rivire	1421-37	
36. Jean de Lastic	1437-54	
37. Jacques de Milly	1454-61	
38. Pierre Raymond Zacosta	1461-67	
39. Jean-Baptiste Orsini	1467-76	
40. Pierre d'Aubusson, Cardinal	1476-1503	
41. Emery d'Amboise	1503-12	
42. Guy de Blanchefort	1512-13	
43. Fabrice del Carretto	1513-21	
44. Philippe Villiers de I'Isle-Adam	1521-34	
45. Pierre del Ponte	1534-35	
46. Didier de Saint-Jaille	1535-36	
47. Jean de Homedes	1536-53	
48. Claude de la Sengle	1553-57	
49. Jean de Valette	1557-68	
50. Pierre de Monte	1568-72	
51. Jean L'Eveque de la Cassiere	1572-81	
52. Hugues Loubenx de Verdala	1581-95	
53. Martin Garzes	1595-1601	
54. Alof de Wignacourt	1601-22	
55. Louis Mendez de Vasconcellos	1622-23	
56. Antoine de Paule	1623-36	
57. Jean de Lascaris-Castellar	1636-57	
58. Martin de Redin	1657-60	
59. Annet de Clermont-Gessan	1660	
60. Raphael Cotoner	1660-63	
61. Nicolas Coroner	1663-80	
63. Adrien de Wignacourt	1690-97	
64. Raymond Perellos y Roccaful	1697-1720	
65. Marc'Antonio Zondadari	1720-22	
66. Antonio Manoel de Vilhena	1722-36	
67. Raymond Despuig	1736-41	
68. Manuel Pinto de Fonseca	1741-73	
69. Francesco Ximenes de Texada	1773-75	
70. Emmanuel de Rohan-Polduc	1775-97	
71. Ferdinand von Hompesch	1797-99	

72. Paul I, Tsar of Russia (*de facto*) 1798-1801	Carlo Candida 1834-45
73. Jean Baptiste Tommasi 1803-05	Philippe di Colleredo-Mels 1845-64
74. Jean-Baptiste Ceschi a Santa Croce 1879-1905	Alexandre Borgia 1865-71
75. Galeazzo von Thun und Hohenstein 1905-31	Jean Baptiste Ceschi a Santa Croce 1871-79
76. Ludovic Chigi della Rovere Albani 1931-51	Antoine Hercolani Fava
77. Angelo de Mojana di Cologna 1962-88	Simonetti (*ad interim*) 1951-55
78. Andrew Bertie 1988-	Jean Charles Pallavicini (*ad interim*) 1988

LIEUTENANTS OF THE GRAND MASTER

LIEUTENANTS OF THE GRANDMASTERSHIP

Innico-Maria Guevara	1805-14
Andrè di Giovanni	1814-21
Antoine Busca	1821-34

Pius Franchi de' Cavallieri
(*during the illness of Grand Master*
Galeazzo von Thun und Hohenstein) 1929-31
Ernesto Paternò Castello di Carcaci 1955-62

An aerial view of Cottonera (Museo dell'Accademia Etrusca, Cortona)

SELECT BIBLIOGRAPHY

Abela, G.F., *Della Descrittione di Malta*, Malta, 1647

Baudouin, J., *Histoire des Chevaliers de l'Ordre de S. Jean de Hierusalem*, Paris, 1624

Boisgelin, L. de., *Ancient and Modern Malta & the History of the Knights* of *Jerusalem*, London, 1805

Bosio, G., *Dell'Istoria della Sacra Religione et Illma. Militia di San Giovanni Gierosolimitano*, Rome, 1594

Brockman, E., *The Two Sieges of Rhodes*, London, 1969

Catalogue of the Records of the Order of St. John of Jerusalem, Malta, 1964

Caoursin, W., *Le Fondement du S. Hospital de l'Order de la chevalerie de S. Jehan Baptiste de Jerusalem. Recueil des hitoriens des croisades*, Paris, 1822

Cavaliero, R., *The Last of the Crusaders*, London, 1960

Cambridge Modern History. vol. III. The Wars of Religion, Cambridge, 1907

Curione, C. S., *Nuova Storia della Guerra di Malta*, (trans. E. F. Mizzi), Rome, 1927

Currey, E. H., *Seawolves of the Mediterranean*, London, 1910

Gattini M., *Sunto Storico del Sov. Mil. Ordine di S. Giovanni di Gerusalemme ovvero di Malta*, Naples 1899

Hughes, J. Quentin. *The Building of Malta 1530-1795*, London, 1956.

Hughes, J. Quentin., *Fortress*, London, 1969.

King, E.J., *The Knights Hospitallers in the Holy Land*, London, 1931

King, E.J., *The Rule, Statutes and Customs of the Hospitallers*, London, 1934

Laking, Sir G. F., *Catalogue of the Armour and Arms in the Armoury, Valetta*, London, *1905*

Mallia-Milanes V., *Venice and Hospitaller Malta 1530-1798*, Malta, 1992

Mifsud, A., *Knights Hospitallers of the Venerable Tongue of England in Malta*, Malta, 1914.

Molle, S., *L'Ordine de Malta: Ia Cavalleria*, Rome, 1928.

Porter, W., *The History of the Knights of Malta*, London, 1883

Pozzo, B. dal, *Historia della Sacra Religione Militares A S. Giovanni Gerosolimitano*, Verona, 1703

Prescott, W. H., *History of the Reign of Philip II*, London, 1855

Il Sovrano Militare Ordine Gerosolimitano di Malta: La Storia, L'Organizzazione, Le Opere Umanitarie, Il Ruolo Generale dei Cavalieri, Rome, 1932

Runcimen, Sir S., *A History ofthe Crusades*, 3 vols. Cambridge, 1951-5

Scicluna, Sir H. P., *The Order of St. John of Jerusalem*, Malta, 1969

Seward, D., *The Monks of War*, London, 1972

Schermerhorn, E. W., *Malta of the Knights*, London, 1929

Taafe, J., *History of the Order of St. John of Jerusalem*, London, 1852.

Ubaldini, U. M., *La Marina del Sovrano Militare Ordine di San Giovanni di Gerusalemme di Rodi e di Malta*, Rome, 1970

Vella, A.P., *Storja ta' Malta*, vols 1& 2, Malta, 1979-81

Vertot, L'Abbe R. de., *Histoire des Chevaliers Hospitaliers de S. Jean de Jerusalem*, Paris, 1725